D1250798

The New Face of
Kampuchea

A photo-record of the
first American visit to
Cambodia since the end
of the war.

Photos by Robert Brown
Text by David Kline

Liberator Press, P.O. Box 7128, Chicago, Il. 60680

HOUSTON PUBLIC LIBRARY

79-124973-3
SSC

915.96
B879

SOCIAL SCIENCES DEPARTMENT
HOUSTON, PUBLIC LIBRARY
500 McKINNEY AVENUE
HOUSTON, TEXAS 77002

RO1137 88227

Copyright © 1979 by Liberator Press

All Rights Reserved.
No part of this publication may be reproduced or transmitted in any
form or by any means, electronic or mechanical, including photocopy,
recording or any information storage and retrieval system without the
prior permission of the publisher.

Library of Congress Catalog Card Number 78-64664

ISBN 0-930720-55-5 (cloth)
ISBN 0-930720-56-3 (paper)

Manufactured in the United States of America

First Edition

Contents

Introduction 1

Impressions 13

The Wounds of War 23

Construction 41

Education and Health 55

Angkor 67

The Cooperative 85

The New
Face of Kampuchea 97

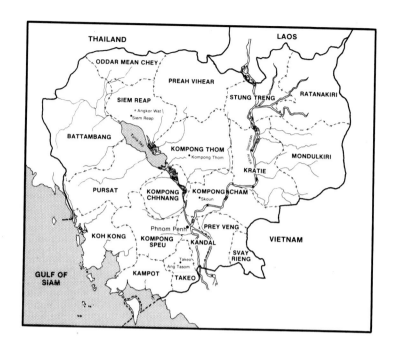

Democratic Kampuchea (Cambodia)

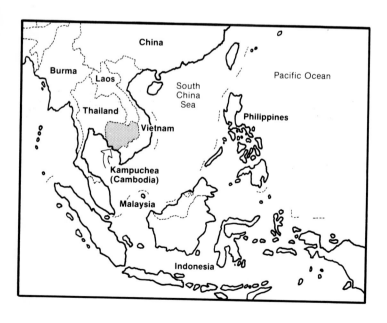

Southeast Asia

Foreword

As this book goes to press, Kampuchea is confronted with a full-scale invasion of her territory by more than 100,000 Soviet-armed soldiers from Vietnam. Their aim is to topple the government of Democratic Kampuchea and install a pro-Soviet, pro-Vietnamese regime in the country.

I witnessed many signs of Soviet and Vietnamese aggression against Kampuchea during my own visit to that country in April 1978. But what I saw was nothing compared to the present offensive.

In light of this new and serious invasion, the publication of this book takes on added significance. Hopefully, the reader will gain a better understanding of the workings of Kampuchean society and see why this small country in Southeast Asia has incurred the hatred not only of the U.S. government, but also of the Soviet colossus that is trying to march across Asia.

David Kline
January 1979

Introduction

On April 12, 1978, we stepped onto the tarmac at Phnom Penh's Pochentong Airport and became the first Americans to visit Cambodia in more than three years. There were four of us, all journalists with *The Call* newspaper, published in Chicago.

No other Americans had set foot in Democratic Kampuchea (Cambodia's official name) since the Revolutionary Army marched into Phnom Penh on April 17, 1975. No other Western journalists had seen the great changes that had taken place since those turbulent days when the U.S. ambassador fled for his life with an American flag clutched under his arm.

Our arrival came at a highly charged moment, politically. Back in the U.S., the press was filled with screaming headlines about "massacres" and "genocide" in Cambodia. President Carter had just called Kampuchea the "number one violator of human rights" in the world.

So we had a great opportunity to investigate previously uncharted ground. What's really happening in Cambodia? What was the internal situation like three years after Kampuchea transformed itself into a socialist society? This was the question we hoped to answer during our stay in that Southeast Asian country.

In all, we spent eight days there, traveling 700 miles across six provinces. We investigated construction

projects, visited rice fields and rural cooperatives, witnessed an electronics school in session, traveled to the world-famous temple of Angkor Wat, and even inspected the border areas where recent fighting with Vietnam had taken place.

We interviewed leaders of the Communist Party and government, including Ieng Sary, Deputy Prime Minister in charge of foreign affairs. And we interviewed many dozens of average citizens, communists and non-communists alike.

We held random discussions with the old and the young, with men and women, in an effort to see how they perceived the Kampuchean revolution. In several cases, we made tape recordings of these interviews and verified the accuracy of the translations made by our government guides once we returned to the States.

To sum it all up, what we saw was a country totally unlike the negative image projected in countless U.S. newspaper articles and television programs. But before going on, a few words about that negative image are in order.

Without a doubt, Kampuchea is today the most maligned nation on the face of the earth. "Genocide," "forced labor," "starvation," "mass executions"—these are just a few of the favorite code words used by the Western press to describe life in Kampuchea today.

These charges (always made by people who have never seen the new society) are reminiscent of the wild slanders which greeted China's liberation nearly 30 years ago. But Kampuchea's leaders are even being accused of actions against their own people which have never before been seen in human history!

A case in point: the CBS Television Network News recently reported *as fact* that a "mating season" has been instituted in Kampuchea. Supposedly, anyone caught "flirting" outside this "mating season" is being executed.

What is CBS's documentation for such an incredible charge? Why, "some refugees told an Illinois Congressman," CBS says, and then this Congressman told CBS!

If a reporter tried to get away with that kind of "documentation" on any other subject, he would be laughed out of the newsroom, and rightly so. But somehow, when it comes to Cambodian horror stories, the requirements of journalistic proof take a back seat to the needs of the anti-Kampuchea propaganda war.

Part of the reason for these rabid attacks on Kampuchea lies in the hostility with which millionaire media magnates—not to mention capitalist governments—generally view socialist revolutions. That is to be expected in any case. But an additional factor here is the desire of the U.S. government to cover up its own role in Kampuchea's recent history.

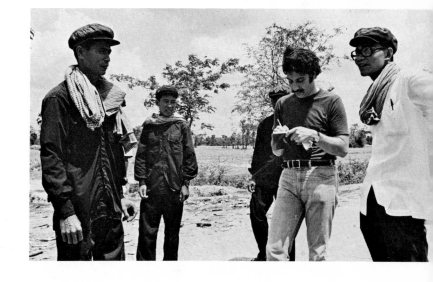

The carnage that was visited on Cambodia in the years before 1975 by the U.S. is now history. The 1970 CIA-directed coup d'état against Prince Norodom Sihanouk which installed Lon Nol in power; the May 1970 invasion by U.S. ground troops that followed; the secret and massive B-52 saturation bombings dating from 1969—all this is conveniently ignored in the slander aimed at Kampuchea today.

Until April 17, 1975, Kampuchea was under the domination of foreign imperialists, especially the U.S.

U.S. advisers controlled Lon Nol's military machine and personally directed the war against the national liberation forces, often referred to in the U.S. as "Khmer Rouge," who were centered in the countryside. Transnational U.S. monopolies like IBM and Esso (Standard Oil) held the jugular vein of the Cambodian economy in their hands.

What about the "independent republic" of Lon Nol? Even many in official U.S. positions have admitted that the Lon Nol regime was merely a creature of the CIA that lacked support among the Kampuchean people. In truth, his regime functioned only to camouflage the fact that all the institutions of society were under the direct command of U.S. officials or their bribed retainers.

Before 1975, the only thing that prevented Lon Nol's overthrow was a powerful military and police apparatus that waged systematic terror against the population. This apparatus was directed from within the air-conditioned offices of the U.S. Embassy on Phnom Penh's Rue Notre Dame.

Inside Phnom Penh, the mansions of the idle rich lay along broad, tree-lined avenues spotted with beautiful teak trees and expansive gardens. Life was indeed a paradise for the upper crust of Kampuchean society and for the U.S. officials who ran things.

But that upper crust was paper thin, eaten away with corruption and hopelessly decadent. Here's a report from the *Baltimore Sun's* issue of April 17, 1975, the very day of liberation:

"For the few privileged elite, the good life of tennis, nightclubs, expensive French meals and opulent brandy-drenched dinner parties went on almost to the very end, while the vast majority of the city's swollen population sank deeper into misery."

As the reporter who wrote that piece indicated, life for most people was something other than a paradise. The capital in the final years and months became choked with 2,500,000 starving refugees made homeless by the U.S. saturation bombings in the countryside. Each morning, "body wagons" picked up the corpses of hundreds of people who had died during the night of starvation, disease or at the hands of Lon Nol's secret police.

That was in Phnom Penh. In the countryside, B-52 bombers piloted by U.S. personnel dropped an estimated 550,000 tons of bombs on Kampuchea in those years, reducing 80% of all the nation's villages to heaps of smoking rubble. Some areas of the countryside took on the appearance of a lunar landscape as a result of the bombings.

By official Kampuchean estimates, 800,000 people were killed; another 200,000 maimed for life. That represents about 12% of the total Kampuchean population, which is a proportional equivalent to 30 million American casualties.

Despite such unparalleled warfare, the U.S. could not destroy the resistance movement. And the Kampuchean guerrillas and their millions of active supporters fought back—sticks against guns, rifles against artillery, and grenades against B-52s. In what was one of the great achievements of human history, this small, poorly armed nation rose up and defeated one of the strongest military powers in the world.

Aside from covering up past crimes, U.S. official-

dom is aiming its propaganda war at the destabilization of the new government. This campaign of slander is combined with CIA-backed coup attempts, border incidents and sabotage.

Additionally, Sen. George McGovern's statement of August 1978, calling for an "international force" to invade Kampuchea is an indicator of the seriousness of U.S. intentions.

The U.S., however, is not the only superpower trying to overturn the Cambodian revolution. The Soviet Union, continuing a quarter century of hostility toward the Kampuchean communists, is even more directly a danger to that country.

In this case, the USSR is the behind-the-scenes instigator of Vietnam's aggression against Kampuchea. Soviet military and logistic support has been an important factor in each of the Vietnamese invasions of Kampuchean territory since December 1977.

With all of this as a backdrop, what exactly is taking place in Kampuchea today?

From all that we saw during our visit, the situation inside Kampuchea is very good. The economy is developing rapidly although still hampered by centuries of underdevelopment. The new government is strong and enjoys broad popular support. And the people are enthusiastically taking part in the revolution with the aim of creating a strong, independent country, free from exploitation and oppression.

We visited the Ang Tasom Cooperative in Takeo Province. There we had a chance to see the Kampuchean revolution played out in detail in the day-to-day life of the masses of people.

"Last year we not only grew enough rice to feed ourselves," a leading member of the cooperative told us, "we also gave the state 10,000 *thangs* (264 tons) of surplus rice. Now everyone has enough to eat and more."

The significance of that statement cannot be emphasized enough. For 2,000 years, Kampuchean peasants have been starving during the dry season. They have historically been at the mercy of both the weather and the landlords, who usually took as "rent" half of what the peasants managed to grow.

Now, however, Kampuchea is self-sufficient in rice. The key factor in this achievement is the destruction of the old feudal and capitalist order. There simply are no more parasitical landlords, and everyone works.

But there's more to it than that. The priority in economic development was and continues to be focused on developing an extensive system of water conservation projects, so that two and three rice crops, instead of just one, can be grown each year through irrigation.

"With water we have rice. With rice we have everything," is the way a popular slogan runs. And literally everywhere we went, we saw people building irrigation canals and dams, often with no tools other than their bare hands.

At Ang Tasom, not everyone among the 1,300 cooperative members works in the rice fields. Some also labor in the wood or metal workshops, where simple agricultural and hand tools are fashioned for the cooperative's own use. With little modern machinery available anywhere in the country due to the years of enforced backwardness, people in each cooperative generally make do with what they can produce themselves.

While inspecting the cooperative's metal workshop, we came across a truly unforgettable sight. In a corner of the work area lay an unexploded 500-pound bomb that had been dropped by a B-52 during the war. Cooperative workers, we discovered, fashion hoes and other metal tools from the melted-down casings of these bombs.

"They dropped so many bombs on us," one of the workers told us, "we're still digging some up that didn't explode."

For us, this was graphic evidence of the tremendous strength and ingenuity of the Kampuchean people. Here they were, the intended victims of U.S. aggression, turning the U.S. government's destructive weaponry to their own advantage.

We asked about the elimination of money. How, for instance, are goods and services distributed?

"The state trucks come here regularly with whatever supplies are available," our host answered, "and we get clothing, sewing machines, cigarettes and other goods not made here at Ang Tasom. In exchange, we load up our surplus rice onto the state trucks for workers in the cities or for needier cooperatives.

"Basically," our host continued, "the people use what they need and give what they can to the cooperative and the state. Our revolution has no model and we are solving the problems we face one by one."

The public health and hygiene of the people has also showed strong improvement in the short span of three

years. Malaria, we were told, has been reduced by 90% through a mass campaign aimed at cleaning up stagnant pools and breeding grounds for mosquitos. We saw no one who appeared sick either at Ang Tasom or any other place we visited.

This improvement in public health has had a sharp effect at the cooperative level. "In March of this year, we had 36 babies born at Ang Tasom," we were told, "and all of them were healthy."

We asked about family life at the cooperative.

"We don't have arranged marriages anymore," one young man told us. "People marry whom they choose." We also found out that family planning is not encouraged because of the country's small population.

Each family has their own home, built on stilts because of the inevitable flooding that occurs during the monsoon season. The houses we saw at Ang Tasom were mostly new, sturdy and attractive, built since liberation in 1975.

"What about the status of women," we asked?

The cooperative leader answered: "Men and women are equal here. They work side by side in the fields, just as they fought side by side during the liberation war. So men have a lot of respect for women."

These were some of the impressions of the new Kampuchea we got at Ang Tasom. But perhaps the most important thing we learned everywhere we went is that most people seem to support the government wholeheartedly.

And why not? From what we could tell, people feel the government not only represents them, but actually belongs to them. A common statement we heard from

people was that their destiny was now in their own hands.

An old peasant put it to us this way:

"The old society was like the darkness . . . . Now, we are working for ourselves, not any masters."

"The revolution has solved the problem of equality for our people," was how another man, a former guerrilla fighter, put it. "We have no more exploitation."

We specifically asked about Western charges of "massacres" after victory in the war. Everyone we talked to denied the existence of widespread killings, and we saw no evidence of "mass executions" ourselves.

If people had been killed in the numbers suggested by the press, surely there would have been some signs, either as physical evidence or in diminished popular support for the government. This was simply not the case.

The people we talked to did not imply, however, that their revolution was accomplished or defended without some bloodshed, especially against counter-revolutionary elements, war criminals and the like.

Party and government leaders, as well as average citizens, stated that violence was needed to break up the entrenched secret apparatus left behind by the U.S.—as well as the Russian KGB—to sabotage the new society and overthrow the government in its infancy. But that violence, we were told, was fundamentally different in nature from that of the U.S. government or its Lon Nol forces. Whatever violence was used after April 17, 1975, was directed towards making sure the broken chains which had previously held the people in bondage would never be forged again.

We realized (and our guides were quick to point out) that Kampuchea is faced with monumental problems in its revolution. For one thing, its economic development must proceed with a practically non-existent industrial base and an agricultural system that is only now reaching stabilization. Kampuchea is still a poor country, even by third world standards, and will remain so for some time.

In our talks with Deputy Prime Minister Ieng Sary, he pointed out that Kampuchea's fundamental orientation in solving its problems is to adhere to the principle of self-reliance. Having made such tremendous sacrifices for their independence and freedom, Kampuchea is not about to lose or barter it away.

Ieng Sary outlined the three fundamental tasks of the nation at this time:

•To defend Kampuchea from any and all attacks and preserve the worker-peasant state power;
•To continue to carry out the socialist revolution by rooting out the remnants of the old exploitative social relations;
•To construct socialism by consolidating an agricultural and industrial base for the rapid development of a modern socialist economy.

One other point should be mentioned about our experiences in Kampuchea. Despite the suffering which the people underwent at the hands of the U.S. government, people were extremely warm toward us, although somewhat shy at first.

One incident particularly moved us. We were talking with some peasants by the side of the road one day. While exchanging ideas, one man said that he regarded the U.S. imperialists, not Americans, as his enemy.

"We know about the students who died at Kent and Jackson universities in America," the peasant explained. "They died for helping our struggle. You must thank the American people for us and tell them we will never forget their aid."

Incredible? We found Kampucheans eager to make friends with the American people, whom they regard as victims of the U.S. policy makers' war on Cambodia, just like themselves.

Although our delegation was the first to visit Kampuchea, we are confident that more Americans will soon be able to go and investigate this new society for themselves. This can only have the effect of giving the American people a more realistic picture of life in the new Cambodia.

In the pages that follow, you will catch a glimpse of a nation reborn, a nation that has "regained its soul," to quote the Kampucheans themselves. We invite you to look through our camera's eye and see the new face of Kampuchea.

David Kline
November 1978

Impressions

14

The scene at left struck us for the contrast—a newly built home in a cooperative surrounded by images of centuries-old peasant life.

With most people we met, the curiosity was mutual. These young women, though shy, were eager to meet the first Americans they knew who had come as friends.

Having heard over the radio that four American friends were touring the countryside, people often gathered around us when we stopped to talk. First ten, then fifty and sometimes hundreds of people would surround us—with the kids, of course, pushing their way up to the front.

Kampuchea's economy is still poor, the result of centuries of underdevelopment. While looking to the time when their agriculture can be mechanized, people today must still rely in most cases on draft animals and hard work to get good rice yields.

Determination and enthusiasm—these qualities account for the rapid progress people are making in building up the country.

Workers at right are constructing an earthen dam about 20 miles up the Mekong River from Phnom Penh. It wasn't unusual to see people competing with each other to see who could get the job done first.

Ieng Sary, Kampuchea's deputy prime minister in charge of foreign affairs, talks with *Call* editor Dan Burstein on April 28, 1978.

Ieng Sary was friendly and down to earth in his manner, and the discussions we had with him helped clear up many of our questions about Kampuchean history and the current state of affairs.

The Wounds of War

To be in Kampuchea today is to be confronted at every turn with the wounds of war.

This used to be the city of Skoun, population about 20,000. Then one day, the U.S. bombers came. We only needed to take these two photographs to capture all that remained after the bombs stopped falling.

Whether it was ruined cities and villages, incinerated forests, or mile after mile of swimming pool-sized bomb craters along the road, the U.S. government has left behind innumerable signs of its aggression.

These scenes brought back many memories.

Like millions of other Americans, we used to watch the six o'clock news each night and see the U.S. efforts at airlifting supplies to Lon Nol's crumbling armies. These U.S. transports are now part of Kampuchea's small air force.

At right is the imposing U.S. Embassy in Phnom Penh. On April 12, 1975, U.S. Ambassador John Gunther Dean sped out of these iron gates under armed escort and made good his escape.

One other note: U.S. officials no longer have to worry about Cambodians illegally parking in front of the embassy.

SI VOUS ETES FATIGUES PENSEZ A CEUX
QUI SONT PLUS FATIGUES QUE VOUS
(AU FRONT)

SAUVEZ NOS FRERES D'ARMES EN
DIFFICULTES PAR VOS INTERVENTIONS
RAPIDES ET DIRECTES AUPRES DASC
OU CCF DE JOUR COMME DE NUIT

កុំមើលងាយកន្ថុយប្បាវ់ ៖ឈបៈបៃ្មុន

ចៀស�a សំនាច ៃខ ក្ដុងៃំ៧ស្បាង

ំ២បត ស្មេះ ៈ ៃ៖ៃៃ្ដួប៍ស្សាង

We visited Lon Nol's War Room in Phnom Penh, preserved exactly as it was found when the Revolutionary Army entered the city on April 17, 1975. Detailed maps showed the position of every guerrilla unit, yet the U.S. and Lon Nol were unable to prevent their own defeat.

To bolster sagging morale in those final days, the generals posted this sign in the War Room (in French!): "If you're tired, think of those at the front who are even more tired."

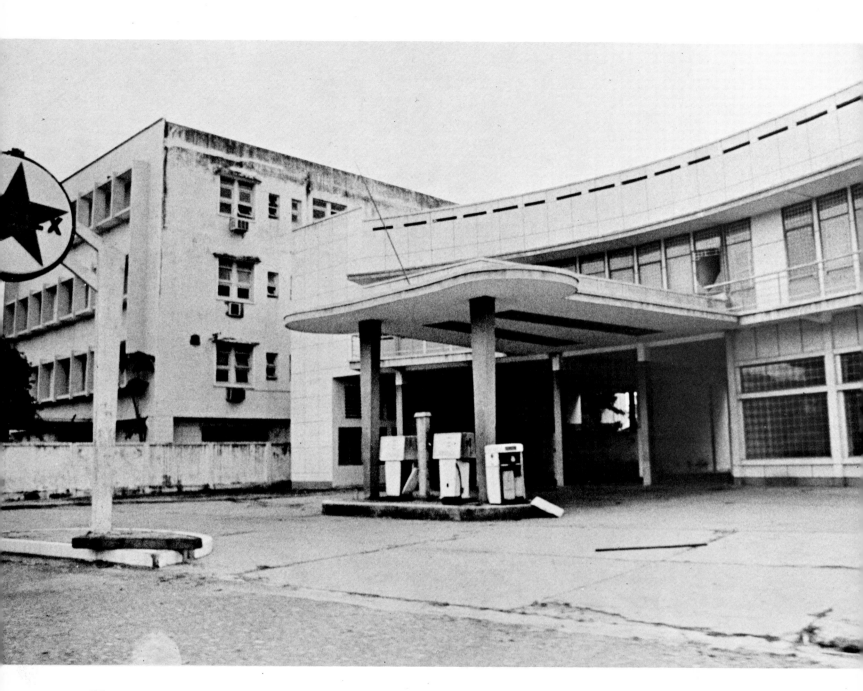

Signs of the former U.S. presence in Kampuchea include the IBM building in a posh downtown neighborhood (at right) and one of many Caltex gas stations.

Many of Phnom Penh's streets, especially in the downtown section, are deserted.

But contrary to the claims of the Western press, the evacuation of the capital was carried out, in the main, through persuasion and for the following reasons:

•When Lon Nol's regime collapsed, there was no food in the city and no way to transport it from the rural cooperatives.

•The U.S., USSR and other governments left behind extensive spy networks to sabotage and hopefully overthrow the new government.

•A mass collective effort was needed to rebuild the agricultural system in the countryside before cities could become viable.

The evacuation of Phnom Penh frustrated the hopes of those who expected the new government to either be starved out or overthrown. Today, 200,000 people live and work in the capital, and more are returning each month.

At right sit the remains of the National Bank of Cambodia. The fact that it was blown up by saboteurs several days after liberation is evidence of the activities of foreign agents.

Work crews (above) have cleaned up most of the filth and rubble of the old city. But still, three years after liberation, some work remains to be done.

The U.S. government continued its war against Kampuchea even after April 17, 1975.

We took these shots in Siem Reap, which was attacked by U.S. F-111 jets flying from bases in Thailand on February 25, 1976—more than 10 months after the war had supposedly ended.

We examined this bomb crater (above) as well as the remains of a school (at right). Twelve children were killed in this school during the U.S. attack.

Since its liberation, Kampuchea has faced attacks from other quarters as well. Vietnam, with support from the Soviet Union, has invaded Kampuchean territory on several occasions and been repulsed each time.

These weapons were captured from the Vietnamese invaders during the December 1977 fighting. Notice the Russian inscription on the rifle scope.

All who supported the struggle of Cambodia and Vietnam against U.S. domination must view this conflict between them as tragic. But from our own investigation, which included visits to battlefields deep inside Kampuchean territory, we had to conclude that Vietnam is the aggressor.

These men and women fighters in the Revolutionary Army described a battle fought at this site, 20 miles from the border with Vietnam.

It was quite a sight to see this young boy carrying an AK-47 rifle not much smaller than himself.

We felt this symbolized the resolve of the people of Kampuchea, young and old alike, to defend their country's independence.

Construction

Everywhere, the face of Kampuchea is being transformed. It was rare to travel more than 30 miles along Highway 7 or 6 and not see another rock-strewn gulley or hillside being reshaped into a rice field, an irrigation canal or a small dam.

Sometimes we would come across a scene of hundreds of people hard at work, like the one at left, where a canal is under construction. The vast majority of building projects we saw, in fact, were devoted in some way to water conservation—the key to a stable agricultural system.

While the obvious enthusiasm of the people was contagious, the work itself was exhausting and hot (the average temperature during our visit ranged over 100 degrees Fahrenheit). As these pictures show, people have to make do with simple hand tools.

This is the January Fifth Dam near the provincial capital of Kompong Thom. In the early 1970s, United Nations "experts" told the government that this dam couldn't be built, owing to engineering problems and a shortage of advanced machinery.

On January 5, 1977, 20,000 people came to the work site here and, in just five short months, built this dam with little more than their bare hands. Here is evidence of the power of self-reliance and mass mobilization.

Throughout their history, the Kampuchean people have alternately faced flood and draught, monsoon and dry season. Today, the problem of maintaining a year-round water supply is being resolved step by step.

Women pull their weight in Kampuchea—even more, in fact, because so many men were killed during the war.

Whether it's backbreaking labor in the fields or construction work previously reserved for men, the women of this new society have taken their place as equals.

Some men still have ideas of superiority over women, we were told, reflecting the feudal traditions of the past. But these ideas are being slowly eliminated, and men are gaining new respect for their female compatriots.

We came across this textile factory (above) under construction near Kompong Thom.

A truckload of curious workers passed us on their way to a job site.

Collective labor rebuilds the country amidst the
ruins of bombed out structures.

Education
and Health

While in Phnom Penh, we visited an electronics training school. Inside these classrooms, we caught a glimpse of the country's future.

After liberation, the Kampuchean people were faced with a huge problem. How would they develop industry, science and technology with almost no

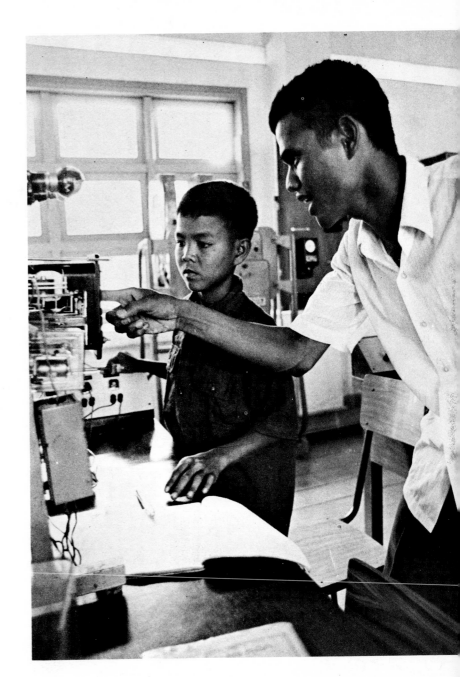

skilled workers or trained scientists? Their answer was to rely on their own resources and learn by doing.

The students, usually between the ages of 10 and 14, study six months and then go to work in factories. Some return for more advanced training.

Maybe because of their youth, the seriousness of these students struck us.

"They are used to taking responsibility," the school's director told us. "Many of their parents are dead and many are also veterans of the *maquis,* of the guerrilla war."

While in many ways, these youngsters are just like kids the world over, they were also forced by circumstance to learn the uses of an AK-47 assault rifle and a well-placed jungle mine.

Before they can learn electronics, these students must first learn to read and write.

Never before in Kampuchean history have the sons and daughters of the poor been allowed to go to school. Now that has changed.

In the three years since liberation, Kampuchea's literacy rate has jumped from 20% to 80%.

You are looking at a pharmaceutical factory in the northern provincial capital of Siem Reap.

At the time of liberation, disease was rampant among the people. Again, this was the legacy of foreign domination and war.

So with few Western drugs available and few people trained in their manufacture, the new government chose instead to rely on traditional medicines used by the peasants.

We saw workers bottling anti-malarial tablets made from the bark of the cinchona tree (the active ingredient is quinine), and were told that most of these traditional drugs were effective in about 80% of the cases. This is somewhat lower than modern drugs used in Western countries.

"But they are better for the people," was how the chief pharmacist put it, "because they are free to all in need. The best drugs in the old society were useless—nobody except the rich could afford them."

Often the new society has to make do with what it has, including the very primitive equipment at left. The soft-drink bottles left by French and American companies are now used to bottle medicines.

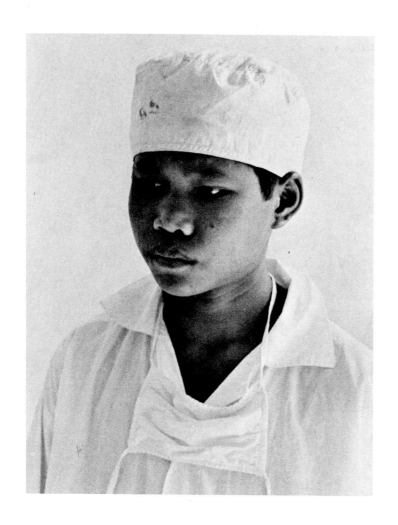

The old teach the young.

Old fighters like this man were once scorned by the ruling classes as "ignorant." Now they are a precious source of knowledge for today's youth.

Angkor

Angkor Wat is one of the world's greatest stone structures, a tribute to the creative skill of the laboring people of ancient Kampuchea.

The largest of an entire complex of temples, Angkor Wat was built between 1113 A.D. and 1152 A.D. by the Khmer King Suryavarman II. It was dedicated as a mausoleum to the god Vishnu.

Early on in the liberation war, the revolutionaries seized Angkor Wat for fear Lon Nol and the U.S. would destroy it. Today, the people recognize this great monument as a national symbol and its yellow image on a field of red makes up the Kampuchean flag.

We walked down this gallery decorated with a bas-relief 300 feet long and were stunned by the intricacy of the carvings. The mythological scenes of war and the capture of prisoners depicted here are more like a living painting than sculpture.

Massive stones were carved and fit into place,
lasting down through the centuries.

U.S. bombers never destroyed Angkor Wat for fear
of world reaction to such a crime. Instead, the U.S.
dropped napalm on the temple in an attempt to kill its
guerrilla defenders. We saw many traces of burned
napalm defacing this monument.

Above, a view from the temple's upper galleries captures some of the lush jungle vastness which surrounds Angkor Wat.

At right are some of the latest hair styles, circa 1150 A.D., for women of the ruling classes.

74

76

At least 150 years before the completion of Angkor Wat, this temple mountain called Takeo was built by Suryavarman I.

Magnificent Bayon—this temple was located at the center of the city of Angkor Thom, ancient capital of Kampuchea. It was built at the end of the 12th century.

The central tower at Bayon, reaching almost 150 feet into the air, features four colossal faces of Bhodisatva (the incarnation of Buddha) carved into it.

Here you can see the religious orientation of most of the temple art. We noticed both Hindu and Buddhist figures, reflecting the competing influences of the two religions.

Of all the temples at Angkor, Bayon captures best the life of its times.

Whether it was the invasion of Angkor by a foreign army or a happy festival scene with all its wit and charm, the bas-reliefs of Bayon made us feel as though we were entering the homes of the common people as they were 800 years ago.

83

The Cooperative

If you want to see what the Kampuchean revolution looks like in day-to-day terms, visit a cooperative. For it is in these rural social institutions that 90% of the country's people live and work.

We paid a visit to the Ang Tasom Cooperative, located in Takeo Province near the border with Vietnam. Here, 1,300 people are pooling their knowledge and skills in a collective effort to develop a prosperous countryside and make a contribution to the nation as well.

Most cooperative residents work in the fields eight hours a day. But Ang Tasom also runs its own metal, wood and other handicraft workshops and produces most of the small tools and equipment it needs.

Workers above are operating a hand-powered wood lathe.

Nothing is wasted at Ang Tasom; everything is turned to good advantage.

At far right is the casing from an unexploded 500 pound bomb dropped by a U.S. B-52 during the war. As the picture shows, the peasants have made hoes from these weapons of destruction.

The other picture at right shows the stacked artillery shell casings picked up from nearby battlefields after Vietnamese troops were driven from the area.

Above is a scene in the metal workshop. Kampucheans, with good reason, have referred to enemy invaders as their "supply sergeants."

It would be a mistake to think that the people live an idyllic existence. The work is hard, and the economy is still underdeveloped.

The kitchen is a very important place in Ang Tasom's scheme of things. We passed through just as the evening meal was being prepared—a meal which included meat, poultry, vegetables and, of course, the staple rice.

"Who does the cooking?" we asked.

"Only those with the highest consciousness," was how one resident answered, reflecting perhaps the importance which a people who not long ago were starving attach to food.

95

This is the cooperative dining hall where people take their meals.

It is also the center of social life, the "town hall," where 1,300 people hold regular meetings to sum up their work and criticize, praise or change the way things are done.

We deeply regretted not being around at the right time to witness and record one of Ang Tasom's mass meetings.

The New Face of Kampuchea

When many of the details of our visit to Democratic Kampuchea have faded, we will still remember the faces.

Here are the faces of a liberated people—of men and women and children who have become the masters of their own country.

photo by D. Kline

103

101

2812-6A
22-90